DATA ALCHEMY

I0500001

TRANSFORMING INFORMATION INTO BUSINESS GOLD

BY

FRED N. PHILLIPS

Data Alchemy

Copyright © 2023 by Fred N. Phillips

Data Alchemy

TABLE OF CONTENT

INTRODUCTION

Amelia was the proprietor of a little but exceptional company as our story begins. She was located in a vibrant metropolis that was home to numerous aspirational businesspeople and forward-thinking leaders. Amelia had a profound comprehension of the significance of information as well as the enormous potential that it offered. She was under the impression that somewhere within the immense amount of data that surrounded her, there were buried treasures just waiting to be found.

Amelia's adventure began when she made an accidental discovery of an old book, a book that was rumored to possess the key to transforming information into unadulterated financial wealth. What is its name? "Data Alchemy: Transforming information into business gold." "Data alchemy." She dove into the ageless wisdom contained inside its pages because she was fascinated by the opportunities that may be found there.

Amelia made a startling discovery while paging through the pages of this incredible book: she came upon a world in which data consisted of more than just numbers and statistics. It was a world in which information possessed a transforming power—a power that could alter the fate of businesses, uncover hidden discoveries, and show the route to achievement. This was a world in which information possessed a transformative power. Amelia went on a journey to become a data alchemist, and along the way, she faced some obstacles and achieved several victories. She became skilled at collecting unprocessed data in a manner like that of an alchemist collecting base metals and refining the information with caution and accuracy. She uncovered the alchemical process of cleaning and preparing data, which involved removing impurities to establish a basis for dependability and precision.

Amelia quickly concluded that the process of transmutation, in which raw data is changed into golden insights, was where the genuine magic of data alchemy resided. She uncovered hidden patterns, made correct forecasts, and gained a competitive advantage by unlocking the power of advanced analytics and harnessing the potential of machine learning and artificial intelligence.

Amelia was able to set off a chain reaction of changes in the company because of her newly acquired skills. She empowered herself to optimize procedures, seize new opportunities, and drive exponential development by adopting a data-driven decision-making philosophy, which became her guiding principle. The universe of data, which had previously been intimidating, turned out to be her ally and guided her toward a future in which innovation and success recognized no limits.

In the book "Data Alchemy: Transforming information into business gold," the author takes the reader on a journey with him or her, during which the reader learns the ins and outs of how data can be transformed into gold. We will investigate the fundamental aspects of data alchemy, become familiar with the alchemical method of deriving useful insights, and gain an understanding of how the transforming potential of data may revolutionize organizations of varying sizes and operate in a variety of fields.

Join me as we go into the world of data alchemy, where we learn to master the art of turning information into pure business gold and unlock the secrets that have been hidden beneath the data mines. Together, we will discover the unrealized potential that is contained within our data-driven future and open the door to new horizons of success and prosperity.

Are you prepared to make the most of this incredible adventure? Let's get started with our investigation of "Data Alchemy: Transforming Information Into Business Gold."

CHAPTER ONE

THE FOUNDATIONS OF DATA ALCHEMY RECOGNIZING THE IMPORTANCE OF DATA IN COMMERCIAL TRANSACTIONS

As a result of the advent of the digital age, data has evolved into a valuable currency in the realm of business transactions. Organizations of all sizes and types, from sole proprietorships to multinational conglomerates, are progressively coming to terms with the essential role that data plays in their day-to-day operations, the processes by which they make decisions, and their overall performance. In the following paragraphs, we will discuss the significance of data in business dealings, focusing on its many facets while also presenting examples from the actual world that illustrate how data may have a substantial influence.

1. The importance of data as a strategic asset:

Data is no longer merely a byproduct of corporate operations; rather, it has developed into a strategic asset that is responsible for driving innovation, growth, and competitiveness. In the interconnected world of today, businesses have access to large volumes of data, which might range from the demographics and preferences of customers to the trends in the industry and the insights gained from finances. Businesses can get useful insights that can help them make important decisions and drive strategic initiatives when they successfully harness and analyze the data they collect.

Take, for example, a business that engages in online retail and collects data on its customers, such as their purchase histories, browsing behaviors, and demographic information. Through the analysis of this data, the firm can obtain a comprehensive insight into the preferences of its customers. This provides the company with the ability to customize product recommendations, improve marketing campaigns, and increase overall customer happiness. If businesses can make strategic use of data, they can gain a considerable advantage over their competitors in terms of recognizing market trends, forecasting consumer behavior, and remaining one step ahead of the competition.

2. Decision-making that is informed by data:
When it comes to business dealings, having accurate data at your disposal is essential for making educated choices. Insights that are generated by data are currently being used to enhance and, in some cases, replace traditional methods that depended on intuition and gut feelings. When businesses analyze their data, they can discover patterns, correlations, and trends that would otherwise remain hidden. This enables businesses to make decisions that are more accurate and evidence-based.

The use of data to drive decision-making can be seen, for instance, in the business world of finance. The identification of possible investment opportunities, the evaluation of risk, and the improvement of portfolio management are all areas in which investment companies rely extensively on data analysis. Investment experts can make well-informed judgments that optimize returns and limit risks by conducting in-depth analyses of huge volumes of financial data, which may include the historical performance of markets, the financials of companies, and economic indicators.

In addition, data-driven decision-making extends beyond the scope of individual transactions and has the potential to have a more far-reaching impact on business objectives. For instance, a retail chain that analyzes its sales data may discover a new market trend that suggests a change in customer preferences. With all of this information at its disposal, the company is in a position to take preventative measures, such as modifying its product offerings or expanding into new areas, to capitalize on the shifting competitive environment.

3. Improving the effectiveness of operations:

Within the context of commercial transactions, data plays an essential part in the enhancement of operational efficiency. Businesses can detect bottlenecks, optimize processes, and streamline operations by evaluating data from their operations, which ultimately leads to cost savings and higher productivity. Take, for example, a logistics company that monitors and evaluates data concerning shipment routes, expenses associated with transportation, and delivery timeframes. By making use of this data, the company can optimize its supply chain by determining the routes that are the most productive, cutting down on the expenses of transportation, and ensuring that deliveries are made on time. The capability to leverage data in this manner can have a substantial impact on a company's bottom line, enabling it to achieve cost reductions and maintain a competitive edge.

In addition, data can be used to improve inventory management if it is analyzed properly. Demand patterns can be recognized by examining previous sales data, which in turn enables businesses to optimize their inventory levels, hence reducing holding costs, avoiding stockouts, and avoiding stockouts. This method, which is driven by data, ensures that firms can meet the demand of their customers while simultaneously decreasing excess inventory and the costs associated with it.

4. Risk management and identifying potential scams:

The utilization of data is critical to the process of minimizing risks and identifying fraudulent activities that occur within the context of commercial transactions. Organizations can identify possible hazards, detect abnormalities, and execute actions to avert financial loss and reputational damage when they analyze data trends and implement sophisticated data analytics methodologies.

For example, to detect fraudulent activity like credit card fraud or money laundering, financial institutions extensively rely on data analysis. By conducting an in-depth analysis of client transaction data, such as spending habits and transaction history, financial institutions can construct sophisticated fraud detection algorithms that are capable of identifying potentially fraudulent activity in real-time. By taking such preventative measures, both the financial institution and its clients are shielded from the possibility of suffering monetary losses.

In a similar vein, data analysis is a very important component in the process of locating possible dangers in supply chains. Businesses can discover possible bottlenecks or weaknesses in their supply chain by evaluating data on the performance of their suppliers, quality control, and delivery schedules. Once identified, the businesses can then take proactive efforts to remedy the issues. This approach to risk mitigation is data-driven, which helps organizations assure a smooth flow of goods and services, avoid disruptions, and keep customers satisfied.

5. Insights from customers and personalized experiences: Data gives organizations the ability to get deeper insights into the behavior, preferences, and wants of their customers, which enables personalized interactions and experiences that are suited to the individual. Utilizing data collected from customers allows businesses to produce more targeted marketing campaigns, provide customers with more personalized product recommendations, and offer superior levels of customer support. Take for example a streaming service that keeps track of the viewing patterns, preferences, and ratings of its users. The service provider can generate personalized suggestions for each user by analyzing this data. These recommendations can propose content that is aligned with the user's interests. The user experience is improved as a result of this level of personalization, which also boosts customer happiness and helps cultivate client loyalty.

In addition to this, data analysis can also be used to assist in locating chances for upselling and cross-selling. Businesses can identify complementary products or services that correspond with the interests and preferences of customers by studying the purchase history of customers as well as their browsing activity of customers. This method, which is driven by data, gives companies the ability to provide customers with tailored offers and recommendations that boost the possibility of making future sales.

6. Considerations of an ethical nature:

While it is important to acknowledge the role that data plays in business transactions, it is also important to address the ethical concerns that are raised by the collecting, storage, and utilization of data. To preserve the trust of their customers and secure their personal information, businesses have a responsibility to ensure openness and comply with any privacy legislation.

As a result of the introduction of rules such as the general data protection regulation (gdpr) and the california consumer privacy act (ccpa), businesses have been put under further pressure to get consumers' consent, protect their data, and give them control over their personal information. Not only does it accord with ethical ideals, but it also contributes to the long-term sustainability and reputation of the company. This is because respecting privacy and using data responsibly helps the long-term sustainability and reputation of the company.

AN INVESTIGATION INTO THE METAPHOR OF ALCHEMY: CHANGING INFORMATION INTO GOLD

The ancient process of alchemy, which consisted of changing base metals into gold, has for a very long time enthralled the human mind. The power of alchemy can be shown to extend beyond the field of chemistry and into many other spheres of existence. This metaphor has continued to be relevant in the present period, particularly in the realm of information and data. In the course of this inquiry, we will investigate the metaphor of ache about the transformation of information into gold. Specifically, we will investigate its importance, practical applications, and examples from the actual world.

A. The meaning behind the alchemical metaphor:

The metaphysical process of transforming something mundane or commonplace into something spectacular and precious is exemplified by the term "alchemy." the phrase "turning information into gold" refers to the process of deriving useful insights, knowledge, and intelligence from raw data. This process is symbolized by the phrase "turning information into gold." individuals and organizations now can unlock the latent potential that is contained within the huge volumes of data that surround us, in a manner that is analogous to an alchemist transforming base metals into gold.

B. The role of data as the primary component:

The transformation of information into gold can be thought of as a metaphorical alchemical process, and the raw material in this process is data. In today's society, we produce an enormous quantity of data from a wide variety of sources, including social media platforms, sensors, financial transactions, and many more. This information, which is frequently referred to as the "new oil," carries an incredible amount of value and potential. On the other hand, in its unprocessed state, it could look chaotic and overpowering. Extracting, refining, and transforming this raw data into meaningful insights and actionable intelligence are the steps that make up the alchemical process.

C. Getting to the bottom of things:

The act of gleaning significant insights from the raw data constitutes the initial stage of the alchemical process. To accomplish this, the data must first be gathered and then organized methodically. Because of advances in technology, we now have access to very effective tools and methods that allow us to rapidly extract insights from data. Natural language processing algorithms, for instance, can examine text data to recognize patterns and feelings. The algorithms that power machine learning can sift through large volumes of data, identify trends, and generate predictions as a result.

D. Refining and filtering:

After insights have been collected, the material must next be refined and filtered before moving on to the next phase. In the same way that an alchemist eliminates impurities from basic metals to purify them, data analysts and scientists eliminate noise and information that is not essential to their work. Following this phase, the future steps will only make use of the data that is the most pertinent to their purposes and correct.

Data Alchemy

When firms refine their data, they are better able to zero in on the essential components that will drive informed decision-making and create value for their businesses.

E. Developing into intelligence that can be put into action: The final step of the alchemical process entails converting the refined insights into intelligence that can be put into action. This is the point at which the metaphor reveals its actual value. Organizations can convert information into knowledge through the processes of analysis, interpretation, and visualization. This knowledge can then be used to drive strategic decisions, innovation, and growth. Businesses can find opportunities, enhance operations, improve customer experiences, and gain a competitive edge when they implement the insights generated from data analysis.

Examples from everyday life:

Let's look at a few real-world examples to explain how the metaphor of alchemy might be applied in the real world:

- Personalization in electronic commerce:

The alchemical process is used by e-commerce systems to transform customer data into tailored recommendations for individual shoppers. Algorithms can recognize patterns and preferences by looking at the browsing and purchasing histories of customers, in addition to demographic information. Following the collection and processing of this data, unique product suggestions, specialized marketing efforts, and individualized user experiences are generated. As a direct consequence, this leads to greater sales as well as enhanced customer loyalty and satisfaction.

- Predictive maintenance in manufacturing:

The alchemical process as seen in the application of predictive maintenance in manufacturing predictive maintenance, which is used in the manufacturing business, is where one can see the alchemical process at work. Manufacturers can discover trends that suggest future breakdowns in machinery by collecting and analyzing data from sensors that are installed in the machinery itself. As a result of translating this data into usable intelligence, firms can schedule preventative maintenance, thereby reducing downtime and increasing operational efficiency.

- Fraud detection in finance:

Financial institutions use the alchemical process to identify fraudulent activity and reduce risks financial institutions use the alchemical process to identify fraudulent activity and reduce risks. Algorithms can detect abnormalities that may signal fraudulent actions such as credit card fraud or money laundering by evaluating transactional data, which includes spending patterns, geographical locations, and odd behaviors. This data-driven method helps protect the institution and its customers from financial losses and helps to retain trust in the institution.

- Healthcare analytics:

In the world of healthcare, the alchemical process is used to extract insights from patient data to improve patient outcomes and increase decision-making. Healthcare analytics is a subfield of data science. Healthcare providers can uncover patterns and correlations by analyzing the data included in electronic health records, medical imaging, and genetic information. This information is then processed into actionable intelligence, which makes it possible to develop individualized treatment regimens, diagnose diseases earlier, and provide superior patient care.

THE CRUCIAL FUNCTION OF DATA ALCHEMISTS IN CONTEMPORARY BUSINESSES

In the world we live in today, which is increasingly driven by data, organizations are becoming more aware of the significance of harnessing the power of data to drive informed decision-making, acquire a competitive edge, and achieve success. This insight has resulted in the establishment of a new role within corporations, which has been referred to as the "data alchemist." in today's modern enterprises, data alchemists perform a critical job by translating raw data into actionable insights. This enables companies to realize the full potential of their data assets. In this piece, we will discuss the function of data alchemists, as well as their talents and responsibilities, and offer concrete illustrations of how these individuals contribute to the flourishing of contemporary enterprises.

- The importance of data alchemists in today's world

Data alchemists are experts who have a unique combination of skills in areas such as data analytics, statistical modeling, data visualization, and domain expertise. Their major responsibility is to collect, refine, and transform raw data into actionable insights that support strategic initiatives and drive decision-making. Data alchemists are skilled in the interpretation of complicated data sets, the recognition of patterns and correlations, and the application of advanced analytics tools to generate intelligence that may be put to use.

- Abilities and obligations:
- Analysis of data: Data alchemists are experts in the process of analyzing massive amounts of data by making use of a wide variety of analytical tools and methods. They have an in-depth knowledge of statistical analysis, data mining, and the algorithms used in machine learning, which enables them to extract significant patterns and insights from the data.
- Data visualization: Data alchemists have a strong understanding of the methods and tools available for data visualization. They can convert extensive data sets into comprehensible visual representations, such as charts, graphs, and dashboards, which make the information much simpler to comprehend and interpret.
- Domain knowledge: Expertise of the domain data alchemists have domain-specific expertise that helps them to contextualize the data and extract relevant insights. This enables them to create value from the data they work with. They have a thorough comprehension of the intricacies and complexity of the market in which they compete, which enables them to recognize important patterns and tendencies that influence the outcomes of business endeavors.

Data Alchemy

+ Skills in communication: Data alchemists are excellent communicators who can explain complicated data concepts to stakeholders who are not technically oriented. They can deliver their results in a manner that is both clear and succinct, making it easier for decision-makers to comprehend and act upon the insights.

Examples of how data alchemists put their skills to work:

- Retail sector: Data alchemists play an essential part in the retail sector, especially when it comes to understanding client behavior and preferences. To find patterns and insights, they analyze consumer data, which includes a customer's purchase history, browsing activities, and demographic information. This information is then put to use in the development of tailored marketing campaigns, the enhancement of product assortments, and an overall improvement in the quality of the experience provided to customers.

For instance, a data alchemist working for an online retailer may examine data about customers to locate a specific group of clients who make frequent purchases of environmentally friendly products. Because the shop is aware of this trend, it can modify its marketing efforts, launch products that are more environmentally friendly, and develop campaigns that are specifically aimed at attracting and retaining this consumer category.

Data Alchemy

- Healthcare industry: Data alchemists play an important role in the healthcare industry, which generates massive amounts of data due to the prevalence of electronic health records, medical imaging, and patient monitoring devices. They do this so that they can see patterns, forecast how the disease will progress, and develop the most effective treatment regimens.

For example, a data alchemist working for a healthcare company would examine the data of patients to determine the elements that play a role in readmissions. The organization will be able to establish ways to prevent readmissions if it first determines the factors that lead to them. Some of these factors include the lack of tailored care plans and inadequate post-discharge assistance.

- Financial sector: Data alchemists are extremely important in the financial sector, particularly when it comes to risk management and the detection of fraudulent activity. They do this by analyzing financial data, which includes the records of transactions, the trends in the market, and the behavior of customers, to identify potential hazards and uncover fraudulent activity.

An employee of a financial institution who works as a data alchemist may examine customer transaction data and detect patterns indicative of probable fraudulent actions. These patterns may include strange spending patterns or unauthorized account access, for example. If the institution can spot these irregularities at an earlier stage, it will be able to take prompt action to both prevent financial loss and safeguard its clients.

- Manufacturing industry: Data alchemists contribute to the manufacturing industry's already high level of operational efficiency and optimization. They do this by analyzing the data that is gathered from sensors, production systems, and the many processes involved in supply chain management to find areas that could be improved, optimize workflows, and cut costs.

A data alchemist working for a manufacturing company, for instance, could examine production data to locate bottlenecks in the manufacturing process. The organization will be able to adopt process improvements, streamline operations, and increase productivity once they have a better knowledge of these constraints.

- The influence that data alchemists have on modern businesses:

The existence of data alchemists within today's enterprises has a significant bearing on the level of success and competitiveness enjoyed by those organizations. Decisions that are data-driven and driven by business objectives can be made by companies by leveraging their skills and knowledge to unlock the value that is hidden inside their data assets and to create data-driven decisions.

i. Improved decision-making: Better decisions can be made because data alchemists give useful insights to organizations data alchemists give organizations useful insights that enable informed decision-making. They enable decision-makers to make evidence-based choices, which optimize operations, drive innovation, and maximize profitability. This is accomplished through the analysis of data and the identification of patterns, trends, and correlations.

ii. Enhanced customer experiences: Data alchemists play a role in the delivery of individualized and specialized consumer experiences. This helps to enhance customer satisfaction. They can comprehend client preferences, anticipate customer demands, and give products that are tailored thanks to the analysis of customer data. This leads to greater customer happiness and loyalty, as well as higher customer value throughout their lifetime.

iii. Efficiency in operational processes: Data alchemists can uncover inefficiencies, bottlenecks, and opportunities for change in existing corporate procedures through the examination of operational data. They assist businesses in achieving higher levels of operational efficiency and productivity by improving workflows, streamlining operations, and cutting expenses.

iv. Risk mitigation: Data alchemists provide a contribution to risk mitigation by doing data analyses to locate potential hazards, vulnerabilities, and fraudulent activities. Their insights make it possible for businesses to put preventative safeguards in place, which in turn protect them from suffering monetary loss, damage to their reputation, and violations of compliance regulations.

CHAPTER TWO

UNVEILING THE ELEMENTS OF DATA ALCHEMY
THE PROCESS OF COMPILING AND EDITING RAW
DATA: MOVING FROM LEAD TO GOLD

Similar to lead in its unprocessed state, raw data does not have much value on its own. On the other hand, by a painstaking process of compiling and editing, it is possible to change it into insightful and useful knowledge, analogous to the alchemical process of turning lead into gold. In this piece, we will investigate the stages involved in assembling and modifying raw data, the significance of this process, and present real-world examples to highlight the transformative power that it has.

The importance of organizing and modifying raw data:

In its unprocessed state, raw data frequently takes on a disorderly, unorganized, and bewildering appearance. It needs to go through a process of compilation and editing before any significant insights can be extracted from it. This process involves acquiring the data, organizing the data, cleaning the data, and refining the data to ensure that the data is accurate, complete, and relevant. Unlocking the actual value of raw data and deriving intelligence that can be put to use requires enterprises to first transform it into a format that is both dependable and usable.

> ➤ First step: collecting and assembling the necessary information:

Raw data must first be gathered and collected before moving on to the next step of the process. These data may originate from a wide variety of sources, including but not limited to customer surveys, transaction records, social media platforms, sensors, or databases maintained by third parties. The objective is to collect as much pertinent data as is practically possible to guarantee a dataset that is complete and accurate.

For instance, a corporation in the retail industry might keep a record of the things bought by customers, as well as the total price of each transaction and the timestamps. They could also collect demographic information such as age, gender, and location if they choose to do so. Businesses can have a comprehensive perspective of their operations as well as their consumers if they collect data from a variety of sources.

➢ The next step is to validate and clean the data:

The raw data frequently consists of errors, inconsistencies, and numbers that are missing. The data will need to be cleansed and validated as the following step in the process to guarantee both its quality and its integrity. This comprises finding and fixing any errors that have been made, getting rid of any duplicates that have been created, and filling in any gaps in the data.

To delete duplicate entries, correct misspelled names or addresses, and check the accuracy of contact details, for instance, data cleaning may be applied to a dataset that contains information on customers. Companies can rely on the data for accurate analysis and decision-making if they take the necessary steps to ensure the data's validity and cleanliness.

Data Alchemy

> ➢ The third step involves the integration and transformation of data.

To make the data easier to analyze after they have been cleaned and validated, they may need to be merged and converted. In this stage, the data from a variety of sources will be combined, the formats will be standardized, and a cohesive dataset will be produced.

For instance, a multinational organization that conducts business in different countries could require the integration of data from a number of its subsidiaries. They can compare and analyze performance metrics across multiple locations, spot trends, and make decisions based on that information because the data have been transformed into a standardized format.

> ➢ The fourth step is to perform an analysis and interpretation of the data.

Now that the dataset has been produced and modified, organizations can move on to the stage where they will analyze and interpret the data. This requires making use of various statistical methods, data mining algorithms, and visualization tools to uncover insights, patterns, and connections.

For instance, a data analyst might use regression analysis to find associations between variables, or clustering algorithms to categorize clients according to their buying patterns. Both of these techniques are examples of data analysis. Through the analysis of the data, firms can unearth previously unknown trends, comprehend the preferences of their customers, and locate chances for growth and optimization.

➢ Reporting and communication, which is the fifth step: The process is not complete until the findings have been presented in a manner that is both clear and succinct. This includes the production of reports, visualizations, and dashboards that can effectively communicate the insights that have been gained from the data.

An example of this would be a marketing team compiling and editing data on the performance of campaigns, consumer interaction, and conversion rates. Then, they can construct a dashboard that gives an overview of the main metrics, which enables stakeholders to rapidly comprehend the impact of marketing activities and make decisions based on the data.

Examples from everyday life:

1. Retail analytics: A significant retail chain gathers and modifies data from a variety of sources, including point-of-sale (pos) systems, customer loyalty programs, and internet transactions. Through the analysis of this data, companies can determine the purchase patterns of customers, improve the efficiency of inventory management, and customize marketing efforts to increase sales.

2. Healthcare research: Data from clinical trials, patient records, and genetic databases are compiled and edited by a healthcare research organization. They can acquire insights regarding the prevalence of the disease, the success of treatment, and genetic markers by examining this data.

Researchers can use this knowledge to build more tailored medicines and get better results with their patients.

3. Financial risk assessment: A financial organization accumulates and edits data from market indexes, economic indicators, and customer financial profiles to determine the level of risk that there. Through the examination of this data, they determine the level of market risk, locate possible instances of credit default, and devise solutions for risk reduction. This enables the institution to make educated decisions about lending, which protects the institution's financial stability.

4. Social media analytics: A social media marketing agency will aggregate and modify data from a variety of platforms, such as engagement metrics, user demographics, and sentiment analysis. This type of work is known as "social media analytics." they can identify customer preferences, monitor brand sentiment, and optimize social media campaigns through the analysis of this data to promote interaction and increase brand exposure.

CLEANING UP THE DATA AND GETTING IT READY FOR ANALYSIS

In this day and age of big data, businesses have access to large volumes of information that, when analyzed properly, can yield useful insights and facilitate the making of well-informed decisions. However, raw data is frequently unorganized, lacking in detail, and inconsistent; hence, a comprehensive cleaning procedure is required to verify the data's quality and dependability. In this article, we will discuss the significance of cleaning up data and getting it suitable for analysis, the difficulties that are involved, and the efforts that businesses can take to guarantee that their data is ready for meaningful analysis. The significance of data cleaning is as follows:

The process of finding and fixing flaws, inaccuracies, and inconsistencies in datasets is referred to as "data cleaning," "data cleansing," or "data scrubbing," and it goes by a few other names as well. It is of critical importance in assuring the quality and dependability of the data, which is vital for proper analysis and decision-making. Organizations can gain relevant insights, recognize trends, and make educated business decisions when they have access to data that has been cleaned.

Obstacles to conquering in data cleaning:

The process of cleansing data is not without its difficulties. When it comes to preparing data for analysis, here are some of the most common issues that organizations face:

✓ Missing data: Data sets often contain missing values datasets frequently contain missing values, which can lead to the introduction of bias and influence the accuracy of the analysis. Some of your data may be from several reasons, including mistakes in data collection, incomplete surveys, or technical problems. When dealing with missing data, careful consideration and the application of appropriate approaches, such as imputation or deletion, are required.

✓ Inconsistent data formats: It is possible to collect data from a variety of sources or to enter it manually, either of which can result in inconsistencies in the data formats. For instance, dates can be written in a variety of forms (such as mm/dd/yyyy or dd-mm-yyyy), and numerical numbers can have a variety of units of measurement depending on the context in which they are used. It is impossible to conduct meaningful analysis or comparison without first standardizing the data formats.

✓ Outliers and anomalies: Outliers and anomalies outliers, also known as extreme values, have the potential to have a major impact on the results of data analysis. These outliers could be the consequence of mistakes in measurement or data entry, or they could be true oddities in the data. It is essential to locate and deal with any outlying do to maintain correct analysis and avoid erroneous conclusions.

✓ Inaccurate or inconsistent data entries: Human errors during data entry might generate inaccuracies or inconsistencies. Inconsistent categorization, misspelled words, and typographical errors are all exampletoin order to guarantee that the data is correct, "data cleaning" involves locating and correcting any errors that may have been made.

The process of cleaning up data

o Auditing and evaluating the data: It is vital to carry out a thorough auditing and evaluation of the dataset before beginning the process of data cleaning. This should be done before starting the procedure itself. This requires an awareness of the data sources, the identification of any potential problems, and the establishment of defined goals for the data cleaning process.

o Handling missing data: There are a variety of methods available for dealing with missing data. Some of these methods include imputation, deletion, and statistical modeling. Imputation is the process of estimating missing values based on already collected data, whereas deletion is the process of eliminating records or variables that have gaps in their associated data. The type of data that is missing and the possible effect it could have on the analysis are two factors that should be considered when selecting a strategy.

o Standardizing data formats: The process of standardizing data formats assures that the analyzed data will be consistent and compatible. This includes converting dates to a format that is standardized, ensuring that the units of measurement are consistent, and standardizing categorical variables so that appropriate comparisons can be made.

o Outlier detection and treatment: Statistical methods such as z-scores, box plots, or domain-specific thresholds can be utilized in the process of detecting and treating outliers. Outliers can be found using these methods. Outliers can, depending on the circumstances, either be eliminated if they are found to be errors or further studied if they are found to represent true abnormalities. When dealing with outliers, significant thought is required to ensure that the dataset's integrity is preserved.

Data Alchemy

- o Correcting inaccurate or inconsistent data inputs: Some number of different approaches that coin order to correct inaccurate or inconsistent data inputs. This may require manually cleaning the data by cross-referencing it with reliable sources, using data validation criteria, or using software tools that can detect and repair common problems.
- o Data validation and quality assurance: Validation of the cleaned data and quality assurance of the data once the initial processes of cleaning the data have been accomplished, it is essential to validate the data to ensure that it is accurate and reliable. This may involve completing data quality checks, cross-checking against reliable sources, and running statistical tests to authenticate the completeness of the dataset.
- o Documentation and version control: It is crucial to keep good documentation of the data cleaning process. This documentation should include the processes followed, the reasoning behind any decisions that were made, and any transformations that were applied. This documentation guarantees that everything is clear and makes it easier to reproduce results. Implementing version control also makes it easier to monitor changes and creates a transparent audit trail that can be referred to in the future.

Some real-world illustrations of how data cleaning works:

a. Cleaning the customer database: To clean up a customer database, a marketing team will detect and remove duplicate entries, validate contact information, fix misspelled names and addresses, and rectify misspelled addresses. This guarantees accurate client segmentation, improved customer relationship management, and targeted marketing efforts.

b. Cleaning up financial data: A financial institution will clean up data relating to financial transactions by locating and correcting anomalies in the data. These inconsistencies may include missing numbers or inaccurate currency codes. This assures accurate financial reporting as well as compliance with regulatory requirements and risk assessments.

c. Cleaning of sensor data: A manufacturing organization will clean up sensor data gathered from production equipment by removing outliers caused by measurement errors or equipment faults. This is done in the process of cleaning sensor data. This ensures that an accurate examination of the performance of the equipment is performed, as well as preventive maintenance and the improvement of the production processes.

IMPROVING THE QUALITY OF DATA: DATA ALCHEMY'S PHILOSOPHER'S STONE

The era of big data has resulted in a deluge of information for businesses, which are struggling to keep up. These data have tremendous untapped potential for fostering insights, creativity, and the making of well-informed decisions. The quality of the data, on the other hand, is what determines its genuine value. In the same way that alchemists looked for a way to turn base metals into gold using the fabled philosopher's stone, modern businesses are on a never-ending hunt for high-quality data, which may serve as a key to unlocking valuable insights and propelling a company's progress toward its goals. In this article, we will discuss the significance of enhancing data quality, the obstacles that businesses must overcome to accomplish this goal, and the methods that data alchemy uses to transform raw data into an asset that can be utilized effectively.

The importance of having good quality data

The terms "accuracy," "completeness," "consistency," and "relevance" are all associated with "data quality." a prerequisite for enterprises to be able to make educated decisions, obtain correct insights, and keep a competitive edge is the availability of high-quality data. On the other hand, having poor data quality can result in faulty analysis, incorrect conclusions, and decision-making that is not well informed. As a result, enhancing the quality of the data is necessary to realize the full potential of the data.

The importance of increasing the quality of data:

- o Reliable decision-making: Making decisions that can be trusted high-quality data can provide a solid basis for decision-making procedures that can be relied upon. Data-driven judgments, which are decisions made by organizations with full confidence because they are based on information that is accurate and dependable, lead to improved outcomes, increased efficiencies, and reduced risks.

Data Alchemy

- Enhanced customer experience: Enhancement of the customer experience gaining a better understanding of a company's clientele is made possible by improving the quality of the data collected. Organizations can create more personalized experiences, deliver targeted marketing efforts, and tailor products and services to fit consumer needs when they have accurate and thorough data about their customers. This ultimately results in increased customer satisfaction and loyalty.
- Efficiency in operations: Having high-quality data makes operations more efficient because it enables more efficient processes and more accurate analysis. Increased productivity, decreased expenses, and enhanced operational performance can be achieved by organizations through the identification of inefficiencies, optimization of workflows, and implementation of data-driven innovations.
- Compliance with rules: Businesses need to ensure that they comply with all applicable data protection rules and sector-specific standards. Compliance with legal and regulatory obligations, including data privacy regulations, financial reporting standards, and industry-specific norms, can be ensured by collecting data of high quality.

CHAPTER THREE

THE TRANSMUTATION PROCESS: FROM DATA TO INSIGHTS

EXPLOITING THE FULL POTENTIAL OF ADVANCED ANALYTICAL TOOLS

In the world we live in today, which is data-driven, corporations have access to massive volumes of data. The ability to extract meaningful insights from these datasets and transform those insights into effective plans is, however, where the true value lies. In this stage of the game, more sophisticated analytic techniques come into play. These tools, which are powered by artificial intelligence and machine learning algorithms, enable firms to discover previously unseen patterns, make accurate forecasts, and gain a competitive advantage. In this article, we will discuss the significance of maximizing the use of advanced analytical tools to their full potential, the benefits these tools provide, and how businesses can make effective use of these tools to generate successful business outcomes.

❖ *The benefits of utilizing state-of-the-art analytical tools:* The term "advanced analytical tools" refers to a collection of technologies and methods that go beyond the scope of traditional data analysis. These tools provide businesses with the ability to discover intricate linkages, recognize patterns, and derive actionable insights from vast datasets including a variety of variables. They do this by employing complex algorithms, statistical models, and machine learning approaches to recognize trends, forecast events, and produce actionable intelligence.

Data Alchemy

Utilizing advanced analytical tools has the following benefits:

1. Making decisions based on data: Modern analytical technologies give organizations the ability to make decisions based on the data they collect. Organizations can obtain a more in-depth understanding of their consumers, the trends in the market, and the performance of their operations if they extract insights from massive amounts of data. Because of this, educated decisions may be made, which in turn leads to enhanced strategies, optimized processes, and improved results.

2. An advantage in the market: Companies and businesses that can make efficient use of more sophisticated analytic tools have an advantage in the market. These technologies can discover patterns in the industry, determine customer preferences, and forecast future demand. With this information, companies may differentiate themselves from their rivals by creating unique products, customizing their marketing strategies, and providing greater experiences to their customers.

3. Enhanced productivity and decreased operating expenses: Modern analytical tools enable businesses to improve their operational efficiencies and cut their operating expenses. Streamlining processes, reducing or eliminating waste, and making educated judgments on resource allocation are all things that may be accomplished by businesses through the analysis of data patterns and the identification of

inefficiencies. This results in an improvement in operational efficiency as well as a reduction in costs and an increase in profitability.

4. Improved customer experience: The use of sophisticated analytical tools enables businesses to obtain a better understanding of the people that make up their clientele. The analysis of customer data, including demographics, behavior, and preferences, enables businesses to create excellent customer experiences, personalize their products and services, and tailor their marketing campaigns to the specific needs of individual customers. This encourages client loyalty, boosts consumer satisfaction, and ultimately leads to increased revenue for the company.

5. Risk reduction: The application of sophisticated analytic methods is an essential component of risk management. The examination of historical data enables companies to recognize patterns and trends that point to the existence of possible dangers. This enables them to implement preventative actions, devise risk mitigation plans, and make decisions based on accurate information, all to reduce risks and avoid future problems.

❖ *Utilizing modern analytical tools to their full potential*: For businesses to make the most of the potential offered by advanced analytical tools, they should consider the following strategies:

Data Alchemy

1) Clearly define objectives: Before using advanced analytical tools, companies need to clearly define their objectives and identify the specific business challenges they want to tackle. This is required to prepare for the implementation of advanced analytical tools. This ensures that the tools are aligned with the strategic goals of the organization and concentrate on the most important aspects of the business.

2) Find sources of relevant data: To provide reliable conclusions, sophisticated analytic tools need access to data that is both of high quality and relevance. The identification and integration of important data sources should be a priority for organizations, to assure data correctness, consistency, and completeness. Methods of data integration and cleaning up the data should be used to guarantee that the data may be used for analysis.

3) Invest in the development of robust analytical models: Organizations should make it a priority to invest in the development of robust analytical models that are adapted to their particular requirements. Performing this step requires picking relevant algorithms and statistical techniques based on the nature of the problem and the data that is available. Data can be analyzed with machine learning algorithms, which can then be used to provide predictions or classifications. Some examples of machine learning algorithms include decision trees, neural networks, and clustering algorithms.

4) Make an investment in data infrastructure: To manage enormous amounts of data and carry out complex computations, advanced analytical tools necessitate the existence of a solid data infrastructure. To facilitate the storing, processing, and analyzing of data, organizations should make investments in scalable infrastructure such as cloud-based platforms or data warehouses.

5) Develop your analytical capabilities: For organizations to make successful use of advanced analytical technologies, they require trained employees who can analyze the data, draw actionable insights, and effectively convey these findings. Investing in the development of an organization's analytical capabilities through the employment of data scientists, the provision of training programs, and the promotion of a culture that is data-driven should be a priority for organizations.

6) Continuously monitor and refine models: To guarantee that they are accurate and relevant, advanced analytical models need to go through a process of being continuously monitored, reviewed, and refined. The performance of the models should be evaluated regularly by organizations, who should then validate their forecasts against the actual results of the world and make any required improvements to increase the models' efficacy.

Some examples of advanced analytical tools include the following:

Data Alchemy

- Predictive analytics: The tools used for predictive analytics make use of data from the past to produce forecasts about potential future occurrences or results. For instance, a company in the retail industry can utilize predictive analytics to forecast client demand, improve inventory management, and organize marketing efforts under those forecasts.

- Natural language processing (NLP): Natural Discourse Processing (NLP) is a term that refers to the use of software tools that enable businesses to analyze and comprehend human discourse. This can be put to use to gain insights from client comments, examine the sentiment of social media, or automate the process of providing customer care with chatbots.

- Algorithms for machine learning: Machine learning algorithms, such as decision trees, random forests, or support vector machines, enable businesses to automate data analysis and produce accurate predictions or classifications. Other examples of machine learning algorithms are support vector machines and random forests. These algorithms have a wide range of potential applications, including the identification of fraudulent activity, the categorization of customers, and the development of recommendation systems.

- Text analytics: Tools for text analytics examine unstructured textual data, such as customer reviews, social media posts, or survey results. Examples of this type of data include. These tools extract useful insights from text data, enabling businesses to comprehend the sentiment of their customers, recognize new trends, or spot abnormalities.

Improvements to the data quality face the following obstacles:

Improving the quality of the data does not come without its share of obstacles. On the path toward collecting high-quality data, organizations must overcome some challenges, including the following:

✓ Data complexity: The complexity of the data stems from the fact that it can be found in a variety of formats and structures and originates from a wide range of places. The process of integrating and standardizing many, unrelated data sets can be difficult and calls for the use of complex tools and methods for data integration.

✓ Data volume and velocity: Both the exponential expansion of data and its real-time nature of it present issues for data management and quality assurance on a large scale. For organizations to effectively manage the volume and velocity of data, they need to implement scalable infrastructure, sophisticated data management systems, and automated processes.

✓ Data governance: It is necessary to put in place efficient data governance practices if one wishes to keep the data quality intact. This includes developing systems for data ownership and accountability, assigning responsibilities for data stewardship, setting data standards, and applying data quality criteria.

✓ Integration of data: Integrating data from many sources and systems has many obstacles and complications that must be overcome to guarantee that the data is accurate, consistent, and comprehensive. To ensure that the quality of the data is preserved throughout the integration process, organizations need to develop effective data integration processes.

Methods to help improve the quality of the data:
The following are some tactics that companies might use to collect data of high quality:

+ Data profiling and assessment: Data profiling and assessment carrying out an extensive data profiling and assessment exercise help detect problems with the quality of the data. Organizations can get insights into data quality concerns and can prioritize improvement efforts after doing an analysis of the features of the data as well as its completeness, consistency, and accuracy.

+ Data cleaning and standardization: The process of finding and correcting flaws, inconsistencies, and inaccuracies in the data is referred to as "data cleaning." this process is followed by the standardization of the data. During this procedure, duplicates are removed, misspellings are fixed, missing values are filled in, and data formats are standardized. This procedure can be streamlined with the use of automated data cleansing technologies and algorithms, which can also increase data quality more effectively.

+ Data validation and verification: Validation and verification of data validation of data guarantees that data complies with previously set quality standards and validation criteria. Validation of data can also be combined with verification. This process involves implementing data validation criteria, completing integrity checks, and checking the data's accuracy through cross-referencing with reliable sources or expert knowledge.

+ Data governance and documentation: Establishing clear roles, responsibilities, and processes for ensuring data quality can be accomplished through the implementation of rigorous data governance principles. The definition of data standards, the establishment of data quality norms, and the guarantee of continuing data quality management are all responsibilities of data governance frameworks. Maintaining transparency and facilitating continuous improvement are both made easier when data definitions, data lineage, and data quality norms are all documented.

+ Monitoring and measuring data quality: Establishing systems for monitoring data quality enables businesses to proactively detect and manage data quality concerns. This is made possible through data quality measurement. Organizations can evaluate progress, identify areas for development, and take remedial steps when the quality of their data is measured against metrics that have been specified.

+ Integration and transformation of data: Making ensuring that data is integrated, harmonized, and converted appropriately and consistently requires having processes for data integration and transformation that are efficient and well implemented. During the data integration process, organizations should make use of powerful tools and methods for data integration to preserve the quality of the data.

+ Training and awareness for data quality: Improving the quality of the data requires first and foremost the cultivation of a data-driven culture inside the company as well as the promotion of data literacy. Employees are more likely to be aware of data quality issues and more likely to feel empowered to participate in efforts to enhance data quality through training and education programs on data quality best practices, data handling procedures, and the significance of data quality provided to them.

UTILIZING ARTIFICIAL INTELLIGENCE AND MACHINE LEARNING IN YOUR WORK

Artificial intelligence (AI) and machine learning (ML) have changed a variety of industries by providing businesses with the ability to automate processes, derive important insights from data, and make well-informed decisions. The applications for artificial intelligence (ai) and machine learning (ml) are quite diverse, ranging from the processing of natural languages and picture recognition to predictive analytics and autonomous systems. In this article, we will discuss the advantages of incorporating ai and ml into your work, the primary uses of these technologies in a variety of business sectors, and how you can effectively harness ai and ml to boost productivity and innovation in your organization.

The following are some of the advantages of utilizing ai and ml:

A. Automation and efficiency: Artificial intelligence and machine learning can automate mundane and time-consuming processes, freeing up human resources to concentrate on more difficult and strategic endeavors. Automating business operations allows companies to improve their productivity, cut down on errors, and more effectively allocate their resources.

B. Data-driven insights: Artificial intelligence and machine learning algorithms can evaluate massive volumes of data, seeing patterns, trends, and correlations that humans may not be able to recognize. Because of this, businesses can get useful insights and make decisions based on data, which ultimately leads to greater performance and competitive advantage.

C. Enhancement of the customer experience: The use of ai and ml technologies allows for the customization of customer experiences, the provision of recommendations, and the provision of individualized solutions. Organizations can conduct focused marketing efforts, improve customer support and service, and build customer loyalty when they have an awareness of the preferences and behaviors of their customers.

D. Analytics predictive: AI and ML algorithms do exceptionally well in predictive analytics, which enables businesses to foresee future trends, anticipate the needs of their customers, and make proactive decisions for their businesses. Many different areas can benefit from the utilization of predictive models, including sales forecasting, demand planning, risk assessment, and fraud detection.

E. Cost reduction and resource optimization: AI and ML technologies can assist firms in optimizing the allocation of resources, lowering expenses, and improving operational efficiency. Cost reduction is also a potential benefit of these technologies. For instance, predictive maintenance algorithms can identify future faults in equipment, which enables prompt maintenance and reduces the amount of time the equipment is out of service.

Applications of artificial intelligence and machine learning across industries:

➤ Healthcare: AI and ML are bringing about a sea change in the healthcare business by making it possible to make more accurate diagnoses, develop more individualized treatment plans, and find new drugs. Chatbots powered by ai can provide round-the-clock assistance to patients, while machine learning algorithms can evaluate medical imaging data to identify anomalies. In addition, predictive models driven by ai have the potential to aid in the early detection and prevention of disease.

➢ Finance: AI and ML are driving a transformation in the financial sector by automating formerly manual processes such as fraud detection, credit scoring, and risk assessment. The use of machine learning algorithms enables the identification of fraudulent transactions and the prediction of creditworthiness from huge amounts of financial data. Chatbots and virtual assistants powered by ai are also being utilized in the financial and insurance industries to improve customer service.

➢ Retail: The retail business is transforming as a result of the application of ai and ml technologies, which are enabling personalized marketing, demand forecasting, and inventory optimization. Customers can receive personalized product choices through recommendation systems that are powered by machine learning algorithms, and predictive analytics can assist merchants in optimizing inventory levels in response to changes in customer demand and market trends.

➢ Manufacturing: Artificial intelligence and machine learning are improving manufacturing processes by making it possible to perform predictive maintenance, quality control, and supply chain optimization. The data collected by sensors can be analyzed by machine learning algorithms, which then make it possible to schedule preventative maintenance. Systems that are powered by ai are also able to analyze production data in real-time, which enables them to identify quality concerns and improve production efficiency.

➢ Transportation and logistics: Artificial intelligence and machine learning play an important part in the transportation and logistics industry by enabling route optimization, predictive vehicle maintenance, and demand forecasting. Machine learning algorithms can evaluate traffic patterns to determine the most efficient delivery routes, while autonomous vehicles and drones powered by ai are now being developed to automate both transportation and delivery.

Utilizing ai and ml to their full potential:

You should think about the following approaches if you want to make efficient use of ai and ml in your work:

i. Define clear objectives: Clearly articulate your goals before beginning to adopt ai and ml technologies, it is important to first clearly articulate the goals you hope to achieve. Determine the particular issues or difficulties that can be resolved by utilizing these technologies, and then establish quantifiable objectives to monitor your progress and evaluate your level of success.

ii. Data preparation and integration: To train and test machine learning models, you will need data that is of high quality, relevant, and well-structured. Methods of data integration and cleaning up potentially need to be implemented to guarantee the accuracy and consistency of the data.

iii. Model selection and training: Determine the ai and ml models to use depending on the data you have available and the goals you want to accomplish. Train the models with the help of data that has been tagged, and validate their performance with the help of relevant evaluation measures. Adjust the parameters of the models as required to get the best possible results from them.

iv. Understanding the interpretability and actionability of AI and ML models: It is important to understand the interpretability and limitations of ai and ml models. It is essential to have the ability to explain and understand the outcomes to win the trust and acceptance of the relevant stakeholders. Make sure that the insights that are produced by the ai and ml models are actionable and in line with the goals that you have set for your company.

v. Continuous learning and development: both ai and ml models can profit from ongoing training and development of their capabilities. To improve the accuracy and efficiency of the models, it is important to track their performance over time, retrain them using fresh data, and take into account any feedback received.

Examples of ai and ml tools include the following:
Tensorflow is a framework for open-source machine learning that was developed by google. Tensorflow is also known as tensorflow. It offers a complete ecosystem of tools and libraries for the construction and deployment of machine learning models, which may include deep learning techniques.

Scikit-Learn is a python package for machine learning that has gained a lot of popularity recently. It gives users access to a large variety of techniques and tools, which may be utilized for activities including classification, regression, clustering, and dimensionality reduction.

Amazon Sagemaker is a fully managed service that enables developers to construct, train, and deploy machine learning models at scale. Amazon sagemaker can be found on the amazon website. In addition to the variety of algorithms that are pre-installed, it also gives you the option to bring in your algorithms.

Ibm Watson is a collection of services and tools driven by artificial intelligence that may be used for a variety of applications including natural language processing, image identification, chatbots, and more. It provides pre-trained models as well as application programming interfaces (apis) for easy integration into a variety of applications.

EFFECTIVELY COMMUNICATING INSIGHTS THROUGH THE USE OF VISUALIZATION TECHNIQUES

In the modern, data-driven world, having the capacity to effectively convey insights is necessary for making decisions, finding solutions to problems, and propelling organizational success. Insights can be gained from the study of data, but it is frequently the visualization of these insights that brings them to life and makes them easier to understand. Through the use of visualization tools, we can display complicated data in a manner that is clear, succinct, and aesthetically appealing. This makes it much simpler for stakeholders to comprehend important messages and take appropriate action. In this piece, we will investigate the significance of effectively communicating insights through the use of visualization tools, talk about the benefits that these approaches bring, and provide some instances of good practices.

The potential of visualization based on data:

The practice of representing data in a visual fashion, such as with charts, graphs, maps, and infographics, is referred to as data visualization. It takes the raw data and converts it into useful and easily understandable visual representations, going beyond simple spreadsheets. Data visualization is a great tool for presenting insights for many reasons, including the following important reasons:

- Simplifying complicated data: Data visualization helps simplify complicated data by transforming it into visual representations that are simpler and easier to comprehend. Even when dealing with massive datasets or sophisticated statistical studies, it enables stakeholders to immediately grasp patterns, relationships, and trends through the use of visualization tools.

- Enhancing understanding and retention: Visuals are absorbed by the human brain more rapidly and effectively than text or numbers alone, which contributes to the improvement of both understanding and retention. When we provide material in a visual style, we engage both the visual and cognitive senses, which ultimately leads to improved comprehension, enhanced memory retention, and enhanced decision-making.

- Finding hidden patterns and insights: The use of data visualization tools can assist in finding hidden patterns, correlations, and outliers that may not be immediately apparent when looking at raw data. When we graphically display data, we can recognize trends, recognize abnormalities, and generate data-driven inferences, which ultimately leads to deeper insights and recommendations that can be put into action.

- Storytelling made easier: The ability to create captivating narratives using data is made possible by visualizations. We can lead stakeholders through a logical development of insights and emphasize the most important results if we organize the data into a narrative that is consistent and makes sense. This element of storytelling amplifies engagement, which in turn makes the insights more memorable and influential.

- Promoting collaboration and alignment: Visualizations provide a common language for communication, making it possible for stakeholders from a variety of backgrounds to grasp and interpret data invariably. This helps to promote collaboration and alignment. It encourages collaboration, makes it easier for teams to have talks, and helps teams align themselves around a shared understanding, all of which leads to more effective decision-making and problem-solving.

It is important to keep the following best practices in mind if you want to express ideas through visualization effectively:

- ✓ Get to know your audience first and foremost: Recognize who your audience is, then tailor your visualizations to meet their specific requirements, preferences, and levels of expertise. Take into account the information they are looking for, their level of experience with data analysis, and the setting in which they will be interpreting the visualizations.

- ✓ Select the appropriate type of visualization: You will want to select the type of visualization that most accurately portrays the data and helps support the insights that you want to communicate. Take into consideration things like the qualities of the data, the correlations you like to emphasize, and the message you wish to convey to the audience. Bar charts, line graphs, pie charts, scatter plots, heat maps, and treemaps are all common types of visualizations.

- ✓ Maintain a focus on simplicity and clarity: To simplify your visualizations, simplify them by concentrating on the most relevant data elements and removing any clutter that isn't necessary. When attempting to guide the viewer's understanding, use labels, titles, and captions that are straightforward and to the point. It is important to steer clear of visual distractions, an abundance of hues, and extraneous frills, as these can conceal insights.

✓ Highlight key insights: Using visual signals like color, size, or annotations, bring the reader's attention to the most relevant ideas that have been uncovered. Use colors that contrast with one another, highlight select data points, and add explanatory notes to draw attention to the most important findings or the primary message.

✓ Implementing intuitive design principles: It is important to implement design principles that improve readability and comprehension. When creating visualizations, you should make sure that the scale and axes are correctly labeled, and you should also offer context and units of measurement when applicable. Make use of data representations that are both consistent and logical, such as plotting time along the x-axis of a line graph. Take accessibility rules into consideration to make sure that the visualizations you create are accessible to everyone and can be used by anyone.

✓ Interactive and exploratory visualizations: When it is acceptable, use interactive visualizations to allow stakeholders to explore the data on their own. The visualization should have interactive components that allow viewers to interact with it, drill down into specific data points, and acquire deeper insights based on their interests. Some examples of interactive elements are tooltips, zooming, and filtering choices.

✓ Test and iterate: Before moving on to the next step, test your visualizations on a sample that is representative of your target audience and collect their feedback. Your visualizations should be iterated and refined based on the input that you have received to ensure that they are clear, usable, and effective.

Techniques of effective data visualization include the following examples:

a. Time-series line chart: A time-series line chart is a useful tool for illustrating changes over a while. For instance, it can be used to visualize the traffic that a website receives for a month, illustrating peak periods and pointing out any trends or irregularities that may exist.

b. Bar chart: A bar chart is an effective tool for analyzing data that requires a comparison of values across a variety of categories. It is possible, for instance, to use it to compare sales data for a variety of product categories or the money earned by many different regions.

c. Heatmap: A valuable tool for illustrating relationships and patterns in massive datasets, a heatmap allows users to visualize the data in a graphical format. It does this by representing values with a color-coding system, which makes it simple to distinguish between high and low values. A heatmap can be used to show the preferences of customers across a variety of product features, or it can be used to indicate areas of a geographical map where customers report a high level of satisfaction.

d. Sankey diagram: A Sankey diagram is a useful tool for visually representing the flow of information and the relationships that exist between various entities. It is possible to use it to illustrate the conversion rates at each level of the funnel or to demonstrate the flow of resources in a supply chain. Additionally, it may be used to represent customer journeys.

e. Interactive dashboards: Interactive dashboards give stakeholders a full view of different representations and allow them to explore data in real-time. Users are given the ability to engage with the data, filter information, and obtain deeper insights through the usage of dashboards, which can integrate multiple types of visualizations such as line charts, bar charts, and maps.

CHAPTER FOUR

THE ELIXIR OF BUSINESS TRANSFORMATION UTILIZING DECISION-MAKING THAT IS INFORMED BY DATA

In the data-driven world of today, organizations have access to massive volumes of data, which they may use to their advantage to make well-informed decisions. Nevertheless, the sheer existence of data is not sufficient on its own. It is the application of these data in the process of decision-making that has the potential to generate good outcomes. Gathering, analyzing, and interpreting data is required to make decisions that are informed by data to obtain insights and direct strategic activities. In this article, we will discuss the significance of making decisions based on data, the advantages of doing so, as well as the most important factors to take into account when putting this strategy into action.

The importance of making decisions that are informed by data:

✓ Decision making that is free from subjectivity: The collection and analysis of data enable one to arrive at decisions that are free from subjectivity. When decision-makers have access to data, it helps them to base their choices on real knowledge rather than depending simply on their intuition or the opinions of others. This lowers the likelihood that decisions will be influenced by biases and ensures that they will be based on evidence.

Data Alchemy

- ✓ Increases in accuracy and precision: The use of data to drive decision-making results in increases in both the accuracy and precision of decisions. When relevant data is analyzed, businesses have the opportunity to discover patterns, trends, and correlations that might not be obvious in any other context. This enables those making decisions to make more exact judgments, which ultimately leads to improved outcomes.

- ✓ Identifying chances for growth and innovation and mitigating risks: Data analysis assists businesses in determining where there are chances for expansion and innovation. Decision-makers can find new paths for the development of their businesses by researching the trends of the market, the preferences of their customers, and the actions of their competitors. In addition, firms can detect potential dangers, take measures to reduce such risks and make proactive decisions as a result of using data analysis.

- ✓ Improving the processes of strategic planning: Effective strategic planning can be improved by using data-informed decision-making. Organizations can analyze market circumstances, review performance indicators, and pinpoint areas in need of improvement when they make use of data. Because of this, decision-makers are given the ability to design solid plans that are sensitive to market changes and aligned with the goals of the firm.

- ✓ Optimizing resource allocation: Insights into resource allocation and optimization can be obtained through data

data can provide insights into resource allocation and optimization. Organizations can pinpoint areas of inefficiency, effectively allocate resources, and prioritize initiatives with the highest potential return on investment when they analyze data. This guarantees that the available resources are utilized effectively and strategically.

Important things to keep in mind for making data-informed decisions effectively:

- Define precise objectives: You need to be very specific when defining the goals of your decision-making process. Determine the precise questions that require an answer as well as the issues that require a solution. This guarantees that the efforts put into data collecting and analysis are focused and in alignment with the outcomes that are intended.

- Ensure that you acquire data that is both relevant and of high quality: You need to make sure that the data you acquire is both relevant and of high quality. Think about the data's origins, the methods of data gathering, and the quality control procedures for the data. The correctness, completeness, and dependability of the data will affect the validity of the judgments that are taken and the insights that are gained.

- Data analysis and interpretation: Perform data analysis on the information that was gathered by utilizing the right statistical methods, data visualization tools, and analytical models. Investigate any patterns, tendencies, and linkages that can provide light on the decision-making process. To draw meaningful conclusions from the data, you will first need to interpret it in the context of your goals and the larger business environment.

- Think about the big picture and leverage domain expertise: Although data is valuable, it is essential to think about the bigger picture and make use of domain expertise. It is not appropriate for data to be the single factor considered when making judgments. To arrive at well-informed conclusions, decision-makers should combine the insights provided by data with their own experience, knowledge, and skill.

- Adopt a data literacy attitude: Encourage a data literacy mindset throughout the company's culture. Data analysis, data visualization, and statistical reasoning are all important data literacy abilities that should be encouraged for employees to gain. Because of this, decision-makers at all levels are allowed to interact with data and participate in decision-making that is informed by data.

- Foster collaboration: To foster collaboration, decision-makers, data analysts, and stakeholders should all be encouraged. Data analysts can deliver insightful information, while decision-makers can provide context and experience in a certain field. The promotion of cooperation enables businesses to ensure that data insights are successfully shared and then incorporated into choices that can be put into action.

Data Alchemy

The following are some advantages of making decisions based on data:

- o Increased quality of decisions: Making decisions that are influenced by data results in increased quality of decisions. Organizations can make decisions that are both more accurate and better founded when they depend on the factual information and insights obtained by data analysis.
- o Increased efficiency and cost savings: Decision-making that is informed by data enables firms to recognize inefficiencies and optimize processes, both of which lead to increased efficiency and reduced costs. Because of this, there is the potential for an increase in operational efficiency as well as cost savings due to the more effective allocation of resources.
- o Gaining a superior position in the market: Companies who can properly exploit data will achieve a superior position in the market. Data provides insights into market trends, client preferences, and the behavior of competitors, allowing businesses to uncover opportunities that are unique to them and differentiate themselves in the market.
- o Better risk management: Improved risk management is the result of firms using data analysis to identify and respond to potential threats. When decision-makers have a grasp of patterns and trends, they are better able to foresee and proactively handle possible difficulties, which in turn reduces the impact that risks have on the company.

- o Increased creativity and adaptability: Making decisions based on collected data encourages creativity and adaptability. Utilizing data effectively enables businesses to recognize developing trends, the requirements of their customers, and gaps in the market, which enables them to quickly adjust to changing conditions and capture new possibilities.

Examples of decisions that were informed by data include the following:

Retailers use data to improve inventory management, pricing tactics, and customer segmentation. Retailers are in the business of selling goods to customers. Retailers can make judgments regarding price, product placement, and marketing campaigns that are guided by data after analyzing sales data, customer behavior, and market trends.

In the healthcare industry, providers use data to improve the results for patients, increase operational efficiency, and cut costs. Decisions on treatment regimens, resource allocation, and preventative care programs can be made by providers that are data-informed if they analyze patient data, clinical research, and trends in the healthcare industry.

Banks and other financial organizations rely heavily on data to make educated decisions regarding lending, risk management, and consumer engagement. Financial institutions can make decisions on loan approvals, investment strategies, and targeted marketing campaigns that are informed by data after analyzing customer data, credit ratings, and market trends.

The manufacturing industry makes extensive use of data to improve the efficiency of production processes, the management of supply chains, and the quality of products. Manufacturers can make decisions on production scheduling, inventory management, and the selection of suppliers that are informed by data after analyzing production data, demand estimates, and supplier performance.

IDENTIFYING PROCESS OPTIMIZATION OPPORTUNITIES

Because of the increasingly competitive nature of the modern business environment, companies are always looking for new methods to improve their operations and increase their efficiency. The optimization of the processes involved plays an essential part in the accomplishment of these goals. It entails examining the processes that are currently in place, locating areas in which they may be improved, and putting into action improvements that will simplify workflows, cut waste, and increase productivity. In this article, we will investigate the significance of locating process optimization opportunities, talk about various methods for determining which parts of a system might need the most improvement, and present some examples of process optimization best practices.

The significance of locating process optimization opportunities includes the following:

i. Improving productivity and efficiency: Identifying opportunities for process optimization enables businesses to streamline workflows, remove bottlenecks, and cut out stages that aren't necessary. The productivity of an organization can be increased, products or services can be delivered more quickly, and resources can be distributed more wisely if the organization improves the efficiency of its operations.

ii. Cost savings resulting from process optimization: In many cases, process optimization will result in cost savings. Organizations can decrease their operational expenses, improve their profitability, and gain a competitive advantage if they identify and eliminate operations that do not add value to their products or services, minimize waste, and improve resource usage.

iii. Enhanced customer satisfaction and quality improvements: Optimising a process can lead to improvements in both the quality of the product and the level of satisfaction it provides to the end user. The ability of an organization to improve the consistency and accuracy of its outputs can be increased through the process of identifying areas for improvement, which can ultimately result in higher-quality goods or services. Customers who feel their needs have been met are more likely to remain loyal, spread positive word of mouth, and contribute to a better reputation for the company.

iv. Agility and adaptability: Organizations can become more agile and flexible in response to shifting market conditions when they identify possibilities for process optimization. Organizations can respond more rapidly to the needs of the market, innovate more effectively, and maintain their lead over the competition when they regularly analyze and improve their processes.

Methodologies for identifying potential opportunities for process optimization:

o Process mapping and analysis: Process mapping is the act of visually portraying a process from beginning to end, including all of the activities, decision points, and interactions that take place along the way. This offers a holistic perspective of the process and assists in locating any bottlenecks, redundant steps, or inefficiencies. The purpose of process analysis is to examine the mapped process to find aspects of the process that could be improved, such as lengthy wait times, needless handoffs, or repetitive operations.

o Value stream mapping: Mapping the value stream is method that can help you find waste and inefficiencies in your operations value stream mapping is a method that can help you find waste and inefficiencies in your operations. It entails charting out the flow of things like supplies, information, and activities from the beginning of a process through to its conclusion. By doing a value stream analysis, businesses can discover non-value-added activities within their operations, such as excessive inventory, rework, or delays, and then put into action improvements that would get rid of waste and make the process operate more smoothly overall.

- o Data analysis: The analysis of data is an extremely important step in the identification of potential opportunities for process optimization. Data that is pertinent to an organization can be collected and analyzed, such as cycle times, throughput, error rates, or feedback from customers, to find patterns, trends, and areas that could use improvement. Discovering insights that can directly process improvement efforts is possible for firms that make use of the tools and techniques offered by data analytics.
- o Process metrics and key performance indicators (KPIS): Establishing process metrics and key performance indicators (KPIS) enables organizations to monitor the performance of their processes and identify areas that need to be optimized. This is made possible via the use of process metrics and KPIS. Organizations can identify inefficiencies in their processes and establish goals for their improvement if they monitor indicators such as cycle time, throughput, mistake rates, and customer satisfaction scores.

The most effective methods for optimizing the process:

i. Engage stakeholders: Involving important stakeholders in the process of identifying opportunities for process optimization is necessary. Stakeholders can include employees, managers, and subject matter experts. They contribute significant insights and expertise of the processes gained from firsthand experience, which enables a full overview of the existing status as well as prospective areas for improvement.

ii. Establish a culture of continuous improvement inside the organization: It is important to foster a culture that is focused on continuous improvement inside the organization. Inspire your workforce to be proactive in identifying and reporting any process inefficiencies or pain points they come across. Employees will be equipped with the appropriate tools and abilities if they are allowed to participate in training and development programs that focus on process improvement approaches like lean and six sigma.

iii. Prioritize opportunities: Not all process optimization opportunities are equal. It is essential to prioritize areas for development based on their impact on the organization's goals, the level of happiness experienced by customers, and the amount of money that may be saved. Carry out an in-depth investigation to establish the order of importance of the optimization opportunities, and then distribute resources by the results.

iv. Implement the lean principles: Lean principles, which were derived from the toyota production system, concentrate on minimizing waste and increasing value as much as possible. The implementation of lean principles, such as just-in-time production, continuous flow, or pull systems, can facilitate the streamlining of operations, the reduction of inventory, and the elimination of activities that do not provide value.

v. Accept automation and technology: Both automation and technology have the potential to make major contributions to the improvement of a process. Analyze the processes in which human operations can be replaced by automated ones, thereby streamlining workflows and improving both accuracy and efficiency. It is possible to enable data-driven decision-making and process optimization by putting the right technological solutions into place, such as workflow management systems or data analytics tools.

Listed below are some examples of opportunities for process optimization:

- Management of the supply chain: Businesses can improve the efficiency of their supply chain operations by lowering lead times, strengthening inventory management, and refining logistics procedures. Implementing a just-in-time inventory system, for instance, can help reduce the expenses associated with carrying inventory while also guaranteeing the timely availability of materials.

- Customer service: Increasing response times, standardizing service procedures, and putting in place self-service options are all examples of ways that the customer service process can be optimized. For instance, putting in place a customer relationship management (CRM) system can make interactions with customers more streamlined and allow for more effective case management.

- Operations in manufacturing: Process optimization in manufacturing might involve reducing setup times, boosting equipment usage, and limiting errors, among other potential improvements. Implementing methodologies such as six sigma can make it easier to locate and get rid of product flaws, which ultimately results in higher product quality and less additional work.
- The use of automation solutions and the streamlining of approval procedures are two ways that financial processes, such as the processing of invoices or the administration of expenses, can be improved upon and made more efficient. For instance, switching to electronic billing and implementing expense tracking software that is fully automated can help enhance efficiency and cut down on processing times.

ESTABLISHING A CULTURE THAT IS DRIVEN BY DATA WITHIN ORGANIZATIONS

In this day and age of big data, businesses have access to large volumes of information that, when analyzed properly, can lead to the creation of insightful and effective strategic decisions. However, the true value of data cannot be achieved until organizations build a culture that is driven by data. Only then can the true worth of data be realized. The development of this culture includes the promotion of a frame of mind in which data is regarded as a valuable asset, the promotion of data-driven decision-making, and the creation of an environment that facilitates the gathering, analysis, and exploitation of data. In this piece, we will investigate the significance of cultivating a data-driven culture within enterprises, talk about the fundamental components of such a culture, and present some models of effective procedures for establishing such a culture in a business.

The significance of developing a culture that is driven by data is emphasized here.

- Making educated decisions: A data-driven culture enables organizations to make educated decisions based on evidence rather than intuition or human biases, which enables organizations to make more effective use of their resources. Organizations can get insights, recognize trends, and conduct options analysis more objectively when they make use of data, which ultimately leads to improved decision results.

- Improved performance and efficiency: When data is at the center of decision-making, organizations can pinpoint inefficiencies, streamline processes, and more effectively allocate resources. This leads to improvements in both performance and efficiency. Through the analysis of performance metrics and key indicators, businesses can identify areas in need of enhancement and make modifications based on the gleaned insights from the data to raise levels of both productivity and efficiency.

- Improved strategic planning: Accurate and up-to-date information regarding market tendencies, customer behavior, and competitor activity is made available by a data-driven culture, which lends support to improvements made to strategic planning. Because of this, businesses can design more robust plans, recognize new possibilities, and effectively respond to shifting market dynamics.

- Innovation and agility: Data-driven cultures encourage a company's employees to be more innovative and agile, which benefits the company overall. Organizations can unearth insights that drive innovation and enable quick adaptation to market developments and consumer needs if they encourage people to examine and evaluate data.

- Accountability and openness: An organization with a data-driven culture fosters a climate that encourages accountability and openness among its members. The collection and analysis of data provide a factual foundation on which to base performance assessments, goal-setting, and the monitoring of progress. Transparency and a sense of ownership and accountability are fostered along with a sense of empowerment when data is made easily available and shared among multiple teams.

The following are essential components of a data-driven culture:

- ❖ Commitment from leadership: Committing leadership is the first step in establishing a data-driven culture. Leaders have a responsibility to advocate for the significance of data, highlight the contributions it can make to decision-making processes, and set a good example by incorporating data into their decision-making procedures.

Data Alchemy

❖ Literacy in data: If you want to build a culture that is driven by data, you need to make sure that your employees have the skills and knowledge necessary to interact with data effectively. Providing staff with the skills to gather, analyze, interpret, and convey insights inspired by data should be a priority for organizations, which is why they should invest in data literacy training programs.

❖ Data infrastructure: A solid data infrastructure is crucial for a data-driven culture. This includes putting into place mechanisms for the collection of data, storage of data, integration of data, and analysis of data. To support decision-making that is driven by data, organizations should make investments in proper data management tools and technology.

❖ Data that is easily accessible: To cultivate a culture that is driven by data, firms need to ensure that their employees have quick and easy access to data. This requires the establishment of data repositories, the implementation of data visualization tools, and the provision of user-friendly interfaces that enable employees to gain access to and study data that is pertinent to their roles and responsibilities.

❖ Collaboration and integration across functions: Collaboration and integration across functions are essential components of a data-driven culture. Businesses need to foster an environment that encourages multidisciplinary teams to work together, share data insights, and collaborate on projects driven by data. This encourages decisions to be made across functional lines and contributes to a better overall grasp of the facts.

The following are some examples of best practices for establishing a data-driven culture:

a. Develop crystal-clear goals: To successfully develop a data-driven culture inside your firm, you must first establish crystal-clear goals. Determine the most important results you want to achieve and make sure they are in line with the organization's long-term objectives. This lays forth a straightforward path for instituting a culture that is driven by data.

b. Communicate the benefits: Make sure that all of your staff is aware of the many advantages that come with having a data-driven culture. Describe how you can use data to make better decisions, increase performance, and contribute to the overall success of both individuals and organizations. Emphasize the value that data can provide to the accomplishment of company goals.

c. Foster collaboration: To foster a data-driven culture, it is important to foster collaboration between the various departments and teams. Develop chances for the sharing of information, collaboration on cross-departmental projects, and combined efforts to analyze data. Inspire your staff to pick up new skills from one another and discuss the approaches that have shown to be most successful.

d. Recognize and celebrate triumphs that outcome from data-driven: Decision-making it is important to acknowledge and celebrate triumphs that are the direct outcome of data-driven decision-making. Showcase some examples of how the utilization of data has resulted in beneficial outcomes, increased efficiency, or improved customer happiness. The significance of data is reaffirmed, and employees are inspired to adopt a mindset that is data-driven as a result of this.

e. Encourage experimenting: To encourage experimenting and learning from data, you should first establish an environment that supports these goals. Inspire your staff to dig into the data, put their hypothesis to the test, and come up with creative solutions based on what they learn. Embrace a mindset that looks at setbacks and mistakes as opportunities for personal growth and development.

Some organizations that have a strong data-driven culture include the following:

✓ Amazon: Amazon has developed a robust data-driven culture and makes effective use of data to further its customer-centric strategy and improve operational efficacy. They can tailor their consumer experiences, optimize their supply chain operations, and drive strategic initiatives thanks to the incorporation of data analysis into their decision-making processes at a deep level.

✓ Netflix: Netflix is well-known for its data-driven culture, in which the company uses data to make data-driven decisions on the creation of content, recommendation algorithms, and user engagement. They have been able to create highly tailored watching experiences thanks to their use of data analytics, which has also enabled them to improve their content library.

✓ Google: The success of google may be traced back to the company's data-driven culture. The development of new products, as well as the algorithms that power their search engines and advertising tactics, are all driven by data analysis. They place a strong emphasis on their staff having data literacy, and they provide thorough training on the analysis and interpretation of data.

✓ Airbnb: Airbnb makes use of data to improve the customer experience, optimize pricing tactics, and better the matching of hosts and guests. They examine massive amounts of data to comprehend the preferences of customers, recognize patterns, and arrive at conclusions that are data-driven to enhance the whole airbnb experience.

CHAPTER FIVE

MASTERING THE ART OF DATA ALCHEMY SURMOUNTING OBSTACLES AND OBSTACLES IN DATA ALCHEMY

The process of changing raw data into meaningful insights and information that can be acted upon is a powerful approach that holds enormous potential for businesses in a variety of different industries. This process is referred to as data alchemy. However, just like any other activity with the potential to transform something, data alchemy comes with its fair share of difficulties and impediments. In this post, we will investigate some of the typical challenges that one encounters along the path to data alchemy and propose techniques for overcoming those challenges. Organizations can unlock the full potential of data alchemy and create significant results by first recognizing the obstacles they face and then addressing those challenges.

❖ Data integrity and quality:

Ensuring that the data is of high quality and integrity is one of the key challenges presented by data alchemy. The presence of errors, inconsistencies, or missing numbers in raw data might result in the generation of insights that are skewed or inaccurate. It is of the utmost importance to put in place procedures and practices for data governance that will guarantee the accuracy, completeness, and consistency of the data. This includes putting in place tests for the validity of the data, procedures for cleaning the data, and effective mechanisms for integrating the data. To keep the data integrity at a high standard throughout time, it is necessary to do quality checks and audits on the data regularly.

❖ Accessibility and availability of data:

Both accessibility and availability of data can be problematic, particularly for businesses that have a variety of data sources and complicated data ecosystems. The smooth integration and analysis of data can be hampered by data that is stored in silos, or fragmented systems, and by data that is stored in different forms or places. Investing in data infrastructure and technologies that enable centralized data storage, rapid data retrieval, and real-time data availability is a requirement for organizations today. It may be necessary in this regard to put into place data warehouses, data lakes, or cloud-based solutions that make data access and integration easier.

❖ Privacy and protection of data:

As data continues to become an increasingly valuable asset, organizations are confronted with growing issues over the privacy and protection of their data. It is necessary to ensure complete compliance with all applicable data protection rules, such as the general data protection regulation (gdpr) or the california consumer privacy act (ccpa). Businesses must put in place comprehensive data security protocols, such as those involving encryption, access controls, and data anonymization methods. Concerns about data privacy should be addressed in data governance frameworks, as should the need to ensure that data is managed ethically and responsibly.

❖ Data complexity and volume:

Data Alchemy

The sheer volume and complexity of data can be overwhelming for firms that are attempting to perform data alchemy. Significant obstacles can be presented by the management of enormous datasets, the handling of unstructured data sources, and the incorporation of data from a variety of sources. The complexity of data is a challenge that can be overcome with the assistance of advanced data management and analytics tools, such as big data platforms, machine learning algorithms, and natural language processing approaches. The successful exploration, analysis, and interpretation of data can also be enabled by investing in data scientists and professional data analysts.

❖ Organizational culture and change management:
To successfully implement a data-driven culture, a transformation in the thinking and behaviors of the organization is necessary. Progress can be slowed down by factors such as a lack of awareness, resistance to change, or cynicism over the value of facts. Businesses must cultivate a culture that encourages data literacy, promotes decision-making that is driven by data, and provides support for ongoing education. Conducting training programs, developing data champions or ambassadors, and spreading the word about the benefits of data-driven techniques are all potential steps in this direction. It is possible to encourage cultural transformation by including stakeholders at all levels of the business, offering regular feedback, and recognizing data-driven wins.

❖ Skill gap and talent acquisition:

Data Alchemy

A big barrier that can be encountered while attempting to use data alchemy strategies is the lack of available skilled data experts. The supply of data scientists, data engineers, and data analysts is frequently insufficient to meet the demand for their services. Organizations have a responsibility to make investments in talent acquisition initiatives, which may include forming partnerships with educational institutions, providing staff with further training, and drawing on the experience of outside parties through the formation of collaborations or consultancy arrangements. To bridge the talent gap and establish an atmosphere that is data-driven and collaborative, it is possible to build cross-functional teams that combine technical skills with domain knowledge.

❖ Data governance and ethics:
Upholding data governance principles and conducting ethical data activities is a necessary steps in the data alchemy process. Organizations must develop transparent policies and procedures for the collection, storage, sharing, and utilization of data. This includes determining who owns the data, establishing guidelines for how long it should be kept, and verifying compliance with both ethical and legal standards. Building trust and confidence is very necessary for successful data alchemy, and transparent data governance standards are the key to doing just that.

Methods to overcome challenges when working with data alchemy:

1. Establish a data strategy: The first step in establishing a data strategy is to develop a thorough data strategy that is

in line with the aims of the business and explains the vision for data alchemy. The data's quality, as well as its accessibility, safety, and governance, should all be addressed by the strategy. Additionally, it should clarify the roles and duties of the various stakeholders that are involved in data management and analytics.

2. Invest in the data infrastructure: Establish a solid data infrastructure and put in place technology that supports the integration, storage, retrieval, and analysis of data. Implementing cloud-based solutions, data integration platforms, and data visualization tools could be necessary steps in this process. A data infrastructure that is both scalable and adaptable can manage massive volumes of data and makes efficient processing of that data possible.

3. Encourage data literacy: Foster data literacy across the organization by promoting data literacy and providing staff with training and resources to do so. It is important to encourage people to build abilities in data analysis, comprehend data visualizations, and evaluate data insights. This enables staff members to make decisions that are informed by data and develop a data-driven culture.

4. Prioritize data governance: Prioritize establishing frameworks for data governance that manage data quality, privacy, security, and compliance is an important part of data governance. Appoint data stewards who are accountable for overseeing and executing the policies governing data governance. Audits and quality checks on

the data should be performed regularly to verify their integrity and trustworthiness.

5. Embrace an agile and iterative approach to problem-solving: When working on data alchemy projects, adopt a more agile and iterative approach. Create simpler, more manageable jobs from more involved projects, and then rank those activities according to their importance to the company. Processes for data alchemy should be continuously evaluated and improved based on feedback and new insights.

6. Encourage collaboration and cross-functional teams: Foster collaboration among departments and teams to encourage cross-functional data sharing and analysis encourage collaboration among different departments and teams to encourage cross-functional data sharing and analysis. To achieve a comprehensive knowledge of data insights and their repercussions, it is important to encourage collaboration between data specialists, subject matter experts, and business stakeholders.

7. Utilize automation and AI: Automate as much of the data processing, analysis, and visualization as possible by utilizing various forms of automation and artificial intelligence (ai) technology. Automation has the potential to lessen the amount of manual labor required, enhance data quality, and speed up decision-making procedures. Ai systems can unearth previously hidden patterns, forecast future trends, and make advice on how to proceed.

8. Create a culture that values data and promotes data-driven: Decision making create a culture that places a high value on data and encourages data-driven decision-making. Open communication, experimenting, and learning from the insights provided by data should be encouraged. Individuals and teams that exhibit data-driven results should be recognized and rewarded for their efforts; this will reinforce the significance of data in driving organizational outcomes.

TRENDS IN DATA SCIENCE AND BUSINESS INTELLIGENCE THAT ARE ON THE RISE

Data science and business intelligence are topics that are always developing, and they are the driving force behind decision-making and innovation in companies across a wide range of industries. In tandem with the progression of technology and the ever-increasing availability of data, new trends are emerging that are reshaping how businesses acquire, analyze, and draw insights from data. In this article, we will investigate some of the emerging trends in data science and business intelligence that are expected to have a large influence on companies in the years to come. These trends are positioned to have a significant impact because they combine two fields: data science and business intelligence.

➢ Explainable AI:

Explainable artificial intelligence (AI) is a term used to describe the process of developing ai algorithms and models that can offer clear and understandable justifications for the judgments and forecasts they produce. There is an increasing need to comprehend the underlying logic and reasoning behind the outputs of artificial intelligence systems as these systems become more complicated. Explainable ai provides businesses with the ability to obtain insights into how ai models arrive at their findings, which helps to establish confidence and makes decision-making easier. This trend is particularly significant in regulated industries, such as healthcare and banking, where explainability is essential for ethical and regulatory considerations.

➢ Automated machine learning (AUTOML):
Automated machine learning, often known as AUTOML, is a growing topic that concentrates on automating the process of developing and implementing machine learning models. Developing machine learning models has traditionally required a large amount of specialized knowledge as well as time-consuming processes, such as feature engineering, model selection, and hyperparameter tweaking. These operations are automated by AUTOML tools, making it possible for individuals with only a basic understanding of ml to construct models in a timely and effective manner. AUTOML makes it possible for businesses to make use of the potential of machine learning and democratize data science across a variety of business processes. It does this by lowering the entry barrier.

➢ Federated learning:
Federated learning is a technique of machine learning that enables models to be trained over distributed devices or edge

devices while maintaining the data's decentralized and secure state. Federated learning is also known as distributed learning. When using federated learning, the process of training takes place locally on each device, and the only updates to the model that are sent to the central server are the aggregated versions. This method overcomes the privacy problems that are involved with the sharing of sensitive material while yet allowing for the utilization of the collective intelligence that comes from a large dataset. Federated learning is especially useful in contexts where it is difficult or impossible to centralize data, such as in the healthcare industry or with the internet of things sensors.

➢ Dataops:

Dataops is a methodology that focuses on the collaboration and integration of teams responsible for data engineering, data integration, and data analysis to streamline the process of delivering high-quality data and insights to stakeholders. Dataops is abbreviated as "dataops." in the same way that devops emphasizes automation, collaboration, and agility in software development, dataops does the same for data operations. A reduction in the number of data silos, an improvement in data quality, an acceleration of data pipelines, and an overall improvement in the efficacy of data-driven efforts are all possible results of a company adopting dataops techniques.

➢ Edge analytics and edge intelligence:

Edge analytics and edge intelligence relate to the technique of doing data processing, analytics, and inference at the edge of the network, which is closer to the data source or end-user device. Edge analytics and edge intelligence are also sometimes referred to as "edge computing." edge analytics provides faster decision-making, reduced latency, and increased data security, which is especially useful in light of the growing number of internet of things (iot) devices and the demand for real-time or near-real-time insights. Edge intelligence enables businesses to derive meaningful insights from data collected at the network's edge, which in turn makes possible autonomous systems, predictive maintenance, and real-time monitoring.

➢ Responsible AI:
The necessity for responsible and ethical ai practices is becoming increasingly crucial as the number of applications that make use of ai grows. Responsible artificial intelligence emphasizes ensuring that ai systems are impartial, fair, transparent, and accountable to their users. It entails tackling difficulties in the design and deployment of artificial intelligence, such as algorithmic bias, data privacy, and ethical considerations. Many businesses are making investments in frameworks and rules that will govern the responsible development and use of artificial intelligence (ai) systems in a manner that is congruent with society's values and regulatory needs.

➢ Natural language processing advancements:
Developments in natural language processing (NLP) natural language processing (NLP) is continuing to make rapid strides forward, spurred by the growing demand for numerous

applications to comprehend and process human language. Recent developments in natural language processing (NLP), such as transformer-based models like bert (bidirectional encoder representations from transformers), have substantially improved the capacities of language comprehension. This has resulted in advances being made in areas such as the translation of languages, the analysis of sentiments, the summary of a text, and chatbots. How businesses engage with textual data is being revolutionized by natural language processing (NLP), which enables more accurate sentiment analysis, improved customer service, and improved decision-making.

➢ Graph analytics:

Graph analytics is a new subject that focuses on analyzing and gleaning insights from interconnected data structures known as graphs. This field is still in its early stages of development. Companies now have the ability, thanks to graph analytics, to unearth previously unknown linkages, patterns, and communities hidden within complicated networks. Particularly helpful applications include social network analysis, recommendation systems, the identification of fraudulent activity, and the optimization of supply chains. Graph analytics is a strong tool that offers businesses, which are dealing with ever-increasing amounts of interconnected data, the ability to comprehend intricate relationships and derive insightful conclusions.

➢ Augmented data management:

Data Alchemy

Augmented data management is a practice that integrates the capabilities of artificial intelligence (AI) and automation with more conventional methods of data management to improve the efficacy and efficiency of data operations. It comprises responsibilities such as data integration, data quality, data categorization, and data governance. Augmented data management technologies make use of machine learning techniques to automate tedious data management processes, improve data quality, and empower users to conduct their self-service data discovery. Augmented data management enables enterprises to speed up the decision-making processes that are driven by data by lowering the amount of human effort that is required and giving intelligent data insights.

➢ Ethical data monetization:

Monetization of ethical data as data continues to be a valuable asset, businesses are looking at new ways to ethically profit from their data while still protecting their customers' privacy and keeping their systems secure. Utilizing data assets to their full economic potential while protecting user privacy and acting per applicable legislation is an example of ethical data monetization. This objective can be accomplished by the utilization of strategies such as data-sharing partnerships, data marketplaces, or the application of privacy-preserving methods such as differential privacy. The ethical monetization of data enables businesses to maximize the value of their data holdings while preserving their relationships of trust with consumers and other stakeholders.

ETHICAL CONSIDERATIONS IN DATA ALCHEMY: THE MORAL COMPASS

The process of transforming raw data into meaningful insights and usable knowledge is referred to as data alchemy. This process carries with it a tremendous amount of potential for businesses to drive innovation, improve decision-making, and better consumer experiences. However, given the increasing prevalence of data alchemy, ethical issues must be placed at the forefront of data-driven processes. In recent years, ethical concerns regarding data privacy, bias, transparency, and accountability have gained popularity. As a result, businesses are being urged to traverse the complicated environment of data alchemy with a strong moral compass to avoid potential ethical pitfalls. In this essay, we will highlight the significance of adopting ethical principles to ensure responsible and sustainable data-driven efforts, and we will analyze the ethical considerations that arise in the context of data alchemy.

a) Protection of individuals' privacy and data security:
 The protection of individual's privacy and the security of their data is one of the most important ethical considerations in the field of data alchemy. Organizations must manage data in a way that is respectful of the privacy rights of persons and protects the personal information that those individuals provide. This requires the implementation of stringent data privacy regulations, the acquisition of informed consent for the collecting and processing of data, and the adoption of adequate security measures to prevent unauthorized access, data breaches,

and inappropriate use of personal data. In addition to ensuring compliance with any data protection rules, such as the general data protection regulation (gdpr) or the california consumer privacy act (ccpa), organizations are obligated to make the safeguarding of customer information a top ethical priority.

b) Transparency and explainability:

When it comes to data alchemy, transparency, and explainability are two of the most important ethical factors. Businesses must understand and explain the elements that drive data-driven decisions as they increasingly implement advanced analytics techniques such as machine learning and artificial intelligence. Black-box algorithms, which lack transparency, can lead to biased outcomes, which can then either reinforce already existing inequities or continue discriminatory practices. Businesses must work toward the adoption of explainable ai systems, in which the decision-making process is auditable, transparent, and open to interpretation. Transparency and explainability assist build confidence among stakeholders, make it possible to make decisions that are both fair and objective and contribute to the identification and resolution of potential ethical problems.

c) Fairness and bias:

The introduction of bias into the data alchemy process can have far-reaching effects, including the continuation of institutional discrimination and the reinforcement of societal imbalances. Both the gathering of data and the process of generating decisions could be influenced by prejudice if certain data sources, algorithms, or human biases were used. To ensure that the data transformation process is conducted fairly, organizations have a proactive identification and mitigation of bias obligation. This requires undertaking detailed bias evaluations, resolving biases in data collecting, diversifying data sources, and evaluating the fairness of algorithms across a range of various demographic groups. In the process of data alchemy, companies, and other organizations should make every effort to eradicate discriminatory results and to promote fairness and inclusivity.

d) Governance of data and accountability:

An efficient data governance system is necessary for the ethical processing of data. To manage the gathering, storing, processing, and sharing of data, organizations need to establish policies, procedures, and frameworks that are crystal clear. Data governance must incorporate data quality, data integrity, and data accessibility to guarantee that decisions driven by data are founded on truthful and dependable facts. In addition, businesses should clearly define roles and duties for data stewardship and oversight, and assign accountability for data governance. Strong data governance frameworks build a culture of accountability within firms, defend against the exploitation of data, and encourage ethical business practices all at the same time.

e) Respecting the autonomy of persons and securing informed consent:

One of the most essential ethical considerations in data alchemy is securing informed consent while also respecting the autonomy of persons. Individuals have the right to receive information that is unambiguous and easy to understand from organizations regarding the collection, usage, and storage of their data. They are required to seek individuals' express consent before processing their data, thereby ensuring that persons are aware of the reason for data collection as well as the potential outcomes of such collection. People should be able to access, modify, and erase any personal information that they have stored about themselves, as well as have the option to opt out of any data collection or processing operations. The trust may be built and ethical ideals can be upheld when users' rights are honored and individuals are given authority over the data that pertains to them.

f) Impact on society and gains for society:
Data alchemy has the potential to have a significant positive impact on society and gain for society. It is important for businesses to think about the wider repercussions that their data-driven efforts will have on society and to work toward producing beneficial results. Assessing the possible societal impact of data alchemy initiatives, locating and reducing any bad outcomes, and ensuring the equal distribution of benefits are all examples of things that fall under the category of ethical issues. Organizations should be aware of the potential dangers that are linked with data alchemy, such as job displacement or privacy infringements, and should proactively handle them to reduce the amount of harm done and increase the amount of benefit contributed to society.

Data Alchemy

g) Sharing and collaborating responsibly with data:
In this day and age of linked data ecosystems, sharing and collaborating responsibly with data is an extremely important ethical consideration. Establishing norms and protocols for data sharing that prioritize data privacy, data security, and the equitable use of shared data is an important responsibility for organizations. To ensure that the rights of data providers are protected, they should make sure that agreements governing the sharing of data express plainly the goals, parameters, and restrictions of data usage. A dedication to shared benefits, openness, and appropriate data management should be at the core of any collaboration between businesses. These ethical values should serve as the foundation.

h) Ethical considerations in data alchemy are evolving:
Ethical considerations in data alchemy are not static; they evolve with technological advancements, changes in societal norms, and changes in regulatory policies. Organizations must do ongoing ethical assessments and adjust their policies and procedures accordingly. This requires undertaking regular ethical audits of the data alchemy processes, seeking external ethical assistance, and keeping up to current on the latest evolving ethical frameworks and best practices. Organizations can ensure that their data-driven projects are in line with societal norms and developing ethical standards if they actively engage ethical considerations and work to address those problems.

CONCLUSION

The book "data alchemy: transforming information into business gold" comes to a close by delving into the transforming power of data in current corporate settings. Throughout this book, we have discussed a variety of subjects that are related to data alchemy. Some of these subjects include: the acknowledgment of the significance of data in business transactions; the metaphor of alchemy and its relation to transforming information into gold; the critical role that data alchemists play in businesses; the procedure of compiling and editing raw data; the process of cleaning data in preparation for analysis; the enhancement of data quality; the utilization of advanced analytical tools; the application of artificial intelligence and machine learning; and Businesses may get useful insights, make educated decisions, and drive growth by understanding the value of data in commercial interactions and then leveraging that data to their advantage to gain those insights. The comparison of alchemy is an effective one that highlights the transforming nature of data as well as its potential to turn knowledge into valuable assets for businesses. The metaphor of alchemy serves as a striking parallel.

By applying their skills, knowledge, and expertise to the process of extracting meaningful insights from raw data, data alchemists play an important part in the operations of modern enterprises. Businesses can transform raw data into a format that is structured and usable, making it suitable for analysis and interpretation after going through the process of compiling and modifying the data.

To conduct an accurate and trustworthy analysis, it is necessary to clean up the data and verify its quality. The integrity of a company's data can be improved and the insights it yields can become more valuable if the company takes steps to eliminate data inconsistencies, errors, and anomalies.

Businesses are given the ability to discover patterns, trends, and links hidden within their data when they make use of sophisticated analytical tools. Businesses can uncover significant insights that can drive strategic decision-making and provide them with a competitive advantage through the use of tools such as data mining, predictive modeling, and pattern recognition.

The powers of data alchemy are significantly improved by the use of several technologies, including artificial intelligence and machine learning. Businesses can now automate processes, acquire deeper insights, and make more accurate forecasts based on massive volumes of data thanks to the technologies available today.

It is essential to properly communicate ideas to motivate meaningful action within businesses. Organizations can show complex data in a way that is visually appealing and easy to comprehend by adopting data visualization tools such as charts, graphs, and interactive dashboards. This helps organizations make better decisions and increases engagement with their customers.

Data Alchemy

Instead of depending entirely on intuition or guesswork, organizations can benefit from making decisions that are data-informed, which helps them to make strategic choices that are founded on objective findings. Businesses can improve their decision-making processes, reduce risks, and maximize performance when they make use of data and analytics. Analyzing data to locate inefficiencies, bottlenecks, and potential improvement areas inside a company's operations is one of the steps involved in identifying process optimization opportunities. Businesses can achieve process simplification, increased productivity, and cost savings when they implement the insights that are produced by data.

It is necessary to develop a data-driven culture to successfully integrate data analytics into the very fabric of a business. Businesses can create an atmosphere in which data is valued, utilized, and leveraged effectively if they promote data literacy, foster a culture of data-driven decision-making, and provide the required tools and resources.

Data alchemy, although it offers a plethora of potential, is not without its share of difficulties and hurdles, which must be overcome. To ensure that appropriate and ethical data practices are being implemented, businesses need to address concerns such as data privacy, ethical considerations, bias, and data governance.

Last but not least, the future of data alchemy is being shaped by developing trends in data science and business intelligence, such as augmented analytics, natural language processing, and ethical data monetization, amongst others. Businesses can remain at the forefront of innovation and make use of the most recent technologies and techniques by remaining informed of current trends and adopting them. This allows businesses to unlock the full potential of their data.

www.ingramcontent.com/pod-product-compliance
Lightning Source LLC
Chambersburg PA
CBHW070434220526
45466CB00004B/1676